DANGEROUS DRUGS

TOBACCO AND NICOTINE

MICHAEL BURGAN

Cavendish Square
New York

Published in 2014 by Cavendish Square Publishing, LLC
303 Park Avenue South, Suite 1247, New York, NY 10010

FIRST EDITION

CPSIA Compliance Information: Batch #WW14CSQ

All websites were available and accurate when this book was sent to press.

Library of Congress Cataloging-in-Publication Data
Burgan, Michael.
Tobacco and nicotine / by Michael Burgan.
p. cm. — (Dangerous drugs)
Includes index.
ISBN 978-1-62712-381-5 (hardcover) ISBN 978-1-62712-382-2 (paperback)
ISBN 978-1-62712-383-9 (ebook)
1. Tobacco — Physiological effect — Juvenile literature. 2. Nicotine — Physiological effect – Juvenile literature. 3. Children — Tobacco use — Prevention — Juvenile literature. I. Burgan, Michael. II. Title.
RC567.B87 2014
613.85—dc23

Editorial director: Dean Miller
Senior editor: Peter Mavrikis
Series designer: Kristen Branch

Photo research by Kristen Branch

The photographs in this book are used by permission and through the courtesy of: Cover photo by © Barnaby Chambers/Shutterstock.com; © Barnaby Chambers/Shutterstock.com, 1; Faure et Blanchard/Photononstop/Getty Images, 4; Antoine Juliette/Oredia/Oredia Eurl/SuperStock, 7; Michael Melford/National Geographic/Getty Images, 9; Blank Archives/Hulton Archive/Getty Images, 11; Joyce Naltchayan/AFP/Getty Images, 12; India Today Group/Getty Image, 15; Staff KRT/Newscom, 19; John Somme/E+/Getty Images, 20; Matt Meadows/Photolibrary/Getty Images, 23; Lyhne/MCT/Newcom, 25; AP Photo/Ariel Schalit, 28; BIOPHOTO ASSOCIATES/Photo Researchers/Getty Images, 30; CMSP/Custom Medical Stock Photo/Getty Images, 32; © Art Directors & TRIP/Alamy, 35; Exactostock/SuperStock, 37; © Angela Hampton Picture Library/Alamy, 39; Fort Worth Star-Telegram/ McClatchy-Tribune/Getty Images, 47; Doug Martin/Photo Researchers/Getty Images, 47; WILL & DENI MCINTYRE/Photo Researchers/Getty Images, 47; Alina Solovyova-Vincent/E+/Getty Images, 48; © CHASSENET/BSIP/age fotostock, 54.

Printed in the United States of America

Contents

CHAPTER ONE

What are Tobacco and Nicotine?

"Come on, take a drag. Just one puff won't hurt you."

"Cigarettes are cool. They make you feel good."

YOU MIGHT HAVE HEARD SOMEONE SAY something like that to you. In most states, you have to be 18 to buy tobacco, the main ingredient in cigarettes. But kids and teens who want cigarettes can usually get them, whether they ask someone older to buy them or take them from an adult. The US government says that about 3,500

Left: Almost all cigarette smokers in the United States took their first puff before they were 18 years old. Teen smokers are also more likely to drink alcohol and try illegal drugs.

kids under 18 try cigarettes each day, and about 1,000 of them will become regular smokers.

So what's the big deal? Isn't smoking cool, as some kids think? And kids can buy candy cigarettes. Doesn't that mean the real thing is okay?

No way. Using tobacco in any form isn't cool or okay, because tobacco is one of the most deadly substances people put into their bodies. About 440,000 Americans die each year from diseases related to using tobacco, mostly from smoking cigarettes. And about five million Americans under 18 years old today will die sooner than they would have if they hadn't smoked cigarettes.

Some of the harmful chemicals in cigarettes are sometimes called tar. Think about the thick, black gooey stuff used to pave roads—that's called tar too. Tobacco tar is just as disgusting and obviously bad for you. Along with the tar is a powerful drug called nicotine. This chemical is a poison; strong doses of it were once commonly used to kill insects. The amount of nicotine in one cigarette is pretty small, but it's enough to make tobacco **addictive**, which means people want to use it more and more. And it's nicotine that makes tobacco so hard to give up, even when smokers and users of smokeless tobacco realize it's not good for them.

The addictive quality of the nicotine in tobacco means many users need a cigarette at the start of the day. This habit may make them even more likely to develop certain cancers than smokers who wait for their first puffs.

Nicotine creates a physical addiction—the body needs the drug to feel normal and pain-free. It's also psychologically addictive—users have a mental craving for tobacco, especially in certain situations. One teen describes how she has one "when I wake up, before or after class, after I shower, before I go to sleep and especially always after I eat." Nicotine is thought to be more addictive than several

Kids, Tobacco, and the Law

For a time, some states allowed the sale of tobacco products to teens under 16. But in 1992, the US government said no one under 18 could buy tobacco, and it required the states to enforce this. Later, several states and towns raised the age to 19, and in 2013, lawmakers in several states made a push to increase the age to 21. The call for raising the age came as studies suggested more teens were beginning to smoke for the first time after several years of declining numbers of young smokers.

powerful illegal drugs, such as cocaine and heroin. That's why that one puff of a cigarette or one **chaw** of smokeless tobacco gets so many kids hooked.

The History of Tobacco

If tobacco and nicotine are so harmful, why are they legal today? The answer lies in the history of the tobacco plant

and the spread of tobacco use around the world. When Europeans first reached North and South America, the tribes they met smoked tobacco, a crop not found in Europe. Indians saw the tobacco plant as a gift from their gods. By exhaling the smoke, the Indians were offering prayers to them. The Indians also thought tobacco could help cure some medical conditions, such as sores on the body. And users felt a boost of energy when they puffed on tobacco in their pipes or smoked cigars.

Growing tobacco is still big business in some states, with Kentucky and North Carolina the leading US tobacco producers.

The Indians, though, did not know the health problems related to smoking or chewing tobacco. Neither did the Europeans who came to the Americas and began to use tobacco, too. Like the Indians, they smoked it in pipes. Some also took **snuff**, a form of tobacco inhaled through the nose. The Europeans also spread the use of tobacco to other continents. Today, the plant is grown in more than 120 countries, and it's the most common nonfood crop in the world.

By the early seventeenth century, tobacco was popular in England, and when English colonists settled in Virginia, they grew it to sell overseas. Tobacco became a big business in other southern colonies as well. It remained a major source of income for many Southern farmers after the American colonies won their independence in 1783. For almost 200 years, the United States led the world in growing tobacco.

While the first smokers usually used pipes or cigars, by the nineteenth century cigarettes were more common. They were easier to carry and use than the other forms of smoked tobacco. They became even more common in the United States when Americans perfected machines that rolled cigarettes, with one machine producing 120,000 every day.

Tobacco companies needed to sell the cigarettes they were churning out in such large numbers. One way to do that was through advertising. Ads for cigarettes suggested that successful men and beautiful women smoked cigarettes, so everyone should. One cigarette brand featured a lone cowboy out in the West on his horse, trying to create an image that smoking was tied to independence and toughness.

Ads for the "Marlboro Man," linking smoking with tough, independent cowboys, first appeared across the United States in 1955.

Joe Camel Bites the Dust

Can a cartoon camel make kids want to smoke cigarettes? The US government thought so, which is why kids today never see ads showing Joe Camel. But during the late 1980s and early 1990s, Joe was featured in many ads for the Camel brand of cigarettes. R.J. Reynolds was the tobacco company that introduced Joe Camel to boost the falling sales of what was once the most popular cigarette in America. Joe was sometimes shown with beautiful women nearby, part of an effort to convince men that smoking made them attractive and cool. The ads were so well known that a 1991 study showed that most kids and teens could recognize Joe, whose face appeared on t-shirts and hats as well as ads. For six-year-olds, Joe was almost as familiar as Mickey Mouse! That fact worried some medical experts. They believed the tobacco company was using the cartoon camel to attract young smokers to their brand. In 1997, the US government said R.J. Reynolds was breaking the law by targeting young people with the Joe Camel ads. The company agreed to stop using them, and all cigarette makers are now prevented from targeting kids with cigarette ads.

US Congressman Henry A. Waxman

Learning the Dangers of Tobacco

The ads combined with the addictive quality of nicotine boosted business for the tobacco companies. By the early 1960s, just over 40 percent of all American adults smoked, and in 1963 they inhaled more than 500 billion cigarettes! But the next year, a report from the US **surgeon general** spelled out the extreme health risks of smoking tobacco. Tobacco companies fought back, denying that there was any proof that cigarettes in particular and tobacco in general caused heart disease and cancer. But in the years since 1964, the evidence has only grown: tobacco is a killer. And the tobacco companies knew it all along.

In 1998, state governments reached a legal settlement with the major tobacco companies. The companies agreed to pay the states more than $200 billion over 25 years to help pay for antismoking and health programs. Tobacco companies also agreed to stop aiming cigarette and tobacco ads at kids. Yet in 2013, kids could still easily get tobacco products. Queenly Amankwah, a Massachusetts high school student, said, "Teens can buy a cigarillo, a cheap cigar that's sold singly, for seventy cents at their local corner store. That's less than a bag of chips. They're packaged to attract youth in bright, sparkly wrappers and come in flavors like grape and cherry. They look like candy."

Tobacco Today

While tobacco use has dropped from its peak, too many adults and kids still light up or take a **dip** of smokeless tobacco. Tobacco even comes in candy-like lozenges you can pop into your mouth. Tobacco companies add chemicals to cigarettes that make them more addictive or easier to inhale. Some of these **additives** are also dangerous. Other companies have introduced e-cigarettes, which don't produce smoke. But these mechanical cigarettes still deliver poisonous and addictive nicotine into smokers' lungs.

In their effort to keep making money off a deadly drug, the tobacco companies spend huge amounts of money on advertising. A 2012 report showed that the major companies pour out $8.5 billion in ads for their product.

One of the oldest additives in cigarettes is menthol. It was first used in 1927. Menthol comes from the peppermint plant and has a cool, soothing effect on the throat. It's used in candies and some medicines, but cigarette companies began adding it to their products so smokers with sore throats would keep smoking. The menthol also covered up the harsh taste of tobacco. People who might not like the taste of regular cigarettes might give those with menthol a try. The minty taste and soothing feel has special appeal to young people. Studies show more first-time and early smokers prefer menthol cigarettes, compared to long-time smokers. And young smokers who choose menthol cigarettes are more likely to become addicted than kids the same age who smoke regular cigarettes. In general, studies show that smokers of menthol cigarettes have a harder time quitting than other tobacco users. In 2009, the US government made it illegal to add flavors to cigarettes to try to appeal to young smokers—but menthol remained a legal additive. Since then, public health groups have fought to have menthol banned, too.

Menthol-Smooth Taste, Deadly Effects

CHAPTER TWO

The Dangers of Tobacco and Nicotine

IT MIGHT SEEM CRAZY THAT PEOPLE would choose to put poisons into their body. Maybe it's because with the first few puffs of a cigarette, they don't feel the harmful effects—though they'll probably start to cough, a sign that tobacco is not doing their lungs any good. And for people who chew or dip tobacco, they probably endured dizziness and nausea the first few times—more signs that tobacco is harming their bodies.

But despite those early warnings of tobacco's poisonous qualities, some users continue smoking or chewing. Why? Maybe it's peer pressure, that sense of wanting to do what other kids do—especially if the supposedly "cool" kids are doing it. That pressure is real, as a 2012 study showed. In some middle and high schools, kids might start smoking if they just think the most popular kids smoke—even if those popular kids don't! Then, the new smokers begin to come under the addictive quality of nicotine, and quitting tobacco use becomes harder and harder.

Let's take a closer look at some of the substances in tobacco that make it so harmful to your health, and their effects on your body.

A Deadly Mix of Chemicals

A cigarette contains more than 7,000 chemicals, and a dip or chaw has many of the same ones. As you read earlier, some of these chemicals are added when tobacco products are made. So what are some of the deadly chemicals you put into your body with every puff or dip?

Formaldehyde – Scientists use this chemical to preserve dead animal tissue. It also turns up in some building products. Studies have shown that high levels of formaldehyde cause cancer.

Lead – For years, paint contained lead, until scientists learned that if small kids ate paint chips, they could suf-

What goes on in the body that makes nicotine users crave more of it? The brain is filled with what scientists call circuits—sort of like the circuits in computers. And just as computers and other electrical devices have wires, scientists talk about the "wiring" in the brain. The brain is wired to experience pleasure when certain chemicals called neurotransmitters enter certain "reward circuits." One of these neurotransmitters related to experiencing pleasure is **dopamine**. Nicotine increases the amount of dopamine that reaches the reward circuits, which is why some people feel good when they smoke. Smokers and smokeless tobacco users need increasing amounts of nicotine to feel the same effects—a condition known as **tolerance**. So users become addicted as they keep seeking to turn on their reward circuits. If they stop using, their bodies and minds respond negatively—a condition called **withdrawal**. They can become irritable, depressed, or unable to sleep soundly. To end those feelings, the tobacco users reach for another cigarette or chaw. But the addiction with tobacco is not just physical. Regular

THE NATURE OF ADDICTION

smokers can begin to feel anxious if they go too long without a cigarette. For some, just the act of taking one out and lighting it begins to soften their cravings, even before nicotine reaches their body.

Smoking gives the brain too much of good thing

The brain rewards some behavior – such as eating when you are hungry or learning a new skill – by releasing dopamine, a chemical that makes it feel good. Nicotine makes the brain release dopamine, and new research found it also interferes with the brain's attempt to turn the feel-good chemical off.

The brain's 'pleasure center'

Two structures control release of dopamine

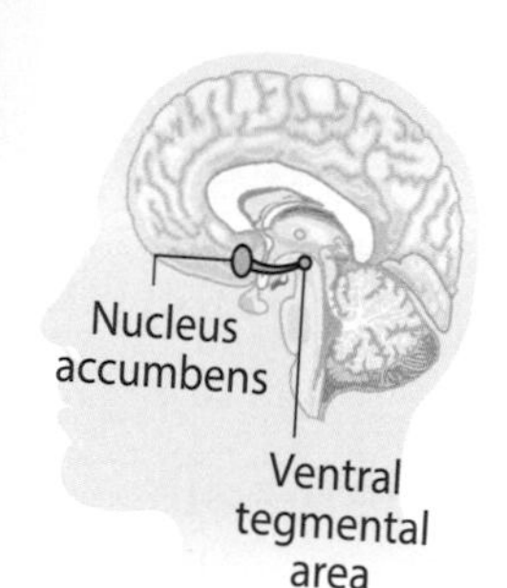

Without nicotine

1 Brain tells reward center to release dopamine to reward a behavior

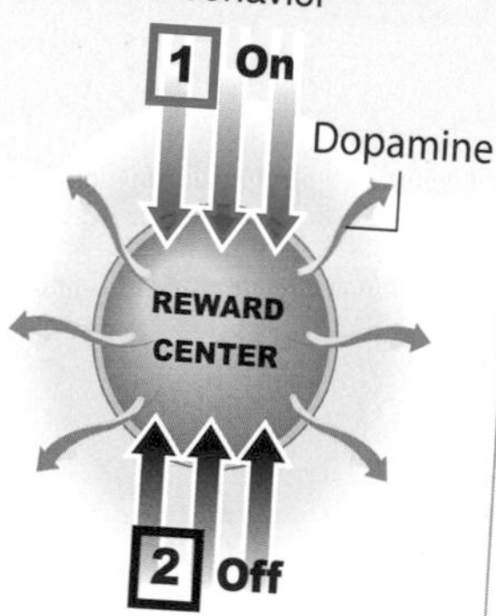

2 Within minutes, the message-carrying chemical acetylcholine turns reward center off

When nicotine interferes

1 With nicotine in bloodstream, reward center releases flood of dopamine

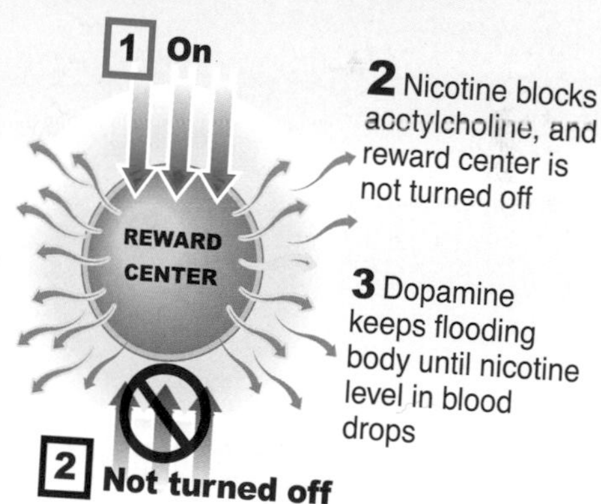

2 Nicotine blocks acetylcholine, and reward center is not turned off

3 Dopamine keeps flooding body until nicotine level in blood drops

4 Brain remembers the pleasurable sensation caused by nicotine and wants more of it – a key factor in nicotine addiction

Source: University of Chicago
Graphic: Lauren Cabell and Phil Geib, Chicago Tribune

Some smokers feel the negative health effects of tobacco but nicotine's addictive quality makes it hard for them to quit.

fer severe health problems. Even adults exposed to lead can have kidney troubles and difficulty learning. Laws got rid of the lead in paint, yet the harmful substance is still in tobacco products—creating health risks for every user.

Cyanide – Spies on secret missions once carried capsules filled with this chemical. If caught, they were supposed to take the cyanide pill, which would kill them almost instantly. That way, they wouldn't be tortured and reveal important information. That same deadly chemical enters your body when you smoke a cigarette.

Carbon monoxide – This "greenhouse gas" comes out of the exhaust of cars and is thought to be playing a part in warming the planet. It's in cigarettes too.

Arsenic – Along with cyanide, cancer researcher Jonathan Winickoff calls arsenic the most dangerous chemical smokers encounter. It's "a poison that is used to kill small

animals," he says. "And there it is in cigarette smoke."

ACETALDEHYDE –Tests on animals suggest that teens are more likely to get hooked on cigarettes than adults, and this chemical may be the reason why. Acetaldehyde makes the addictive qualities of nicotine even stronger, and it seems to have more impact on young, rather than adult, brains.

That First Puff

The various chemicals in tobacco begin to affect the body with a new smoker's first puff. It takes only seconds for the nicotine to reach the brain, and it also stimulates the adrenal glands, which sit near the kidneys. These glands produce the chemical adrenaline, which provides a chemical rush throughout the body. Adrenaline causes deeper and faster breaths, a rise in blood pressure, and a faster heart beat. Those effects of adrenaline are sometimes needed, when a person faces a crisis. The body then prepares for fight-or-flight, or to stand and face the danger or to run away. The adrenaline gives the body the boost of energy it needs in that moment. But constantly triggering adrenaline, as nicotine does, wears out the heart and the **circulatory system**. That first puff and the ones after also boost levels of sugar in the blood. This condition, called hyperglycemia,

is a main symptom of the disease diabetes, and tobacco use increases the chances of developing it.

Nicotine isn't the only chemical with an immediate, negative effect on the body. Harmful chemicals known collectively as polycyclic aromatic hydrocarbons (PAH) begin to have an impact after just 30 minutes of smoking. PAH creates a harmful substance in the bloodstream that can damage **DNA**, which increases the risk of lung and other forms of cancer.

For tobacco users who think pipes, cigars, or chaws are safer, they're kidding themselves. Nicotine and other chemicals don't reach the brain and other parts of the body as quickly as they do with cigarette smoke. But they still have the same harmful effects. And chewing tobacco increases the risk of certain health problems not as commonly associated with cigarettes, as you'll see below.

Long-Term Effects

The real danger of tobacco use comes with how it damages the body over time. Tobacco addicts can't easily quit, even if they want to. Meanwhile, they're damaging almost every organ in their bodies. Here's a look at some of the major parts of the body affected by smoking cigarettes.

The Lungs and Respiratory System

Take a deep drag off a cigarette, and the smoke passes through the respiratory system. That system brings oxygen into the body, which you need to live, and exhales carbon dioxide. The respiratory system is made up of the nose, mouth, throat, trachea, and lungs. Not surprisingly, the toxins in cigarettes are linked to almost all cases of lung cancer in the United States, and lung cancer is the country's deadliest form of the disease.

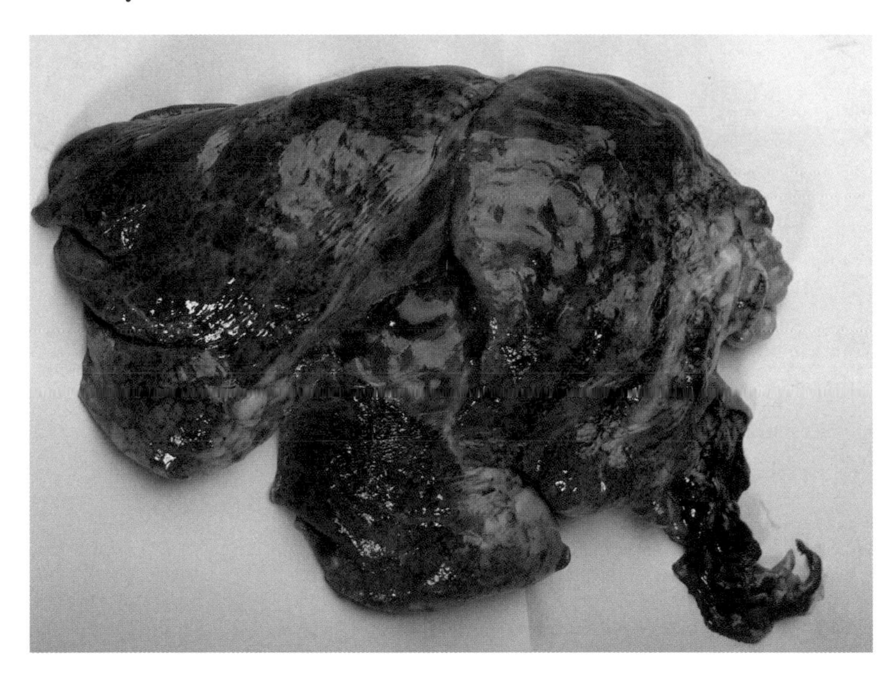

This lung belonged to a person who had emphysema. A healthy lung is reddish pink, not dark like this.

Many of the poisons in tobacco are **carcinogens**, which means they increase the risk of developing some form of cancer. Cigarette's carcinogens are also linked to cancers in other parts of the respiratory system—the mouth and throat. But even if smokers don't develop cancer from their addiction, they face a host of other health problems:

- Worsening of asthma symptoms in people who already have that condition.
- Higher risk of such lung diseases as pneumonia, chronic bronchitis, and emphysema; these last two are sometimes called chronic obstructive pulmonary disease, and about 90 percent of the people who die from it are cigarette smokers.
- More infections in the sinuses, nose, and mouth.
- Constant coughing, to try to clear the increased amounts of mucus that collects in smokers' lungs.
- Difficulty in playing sports or performing other physical activities, since the body needs more oxygen when exercising, and smoking makes the lungs not work as efficiently.

• Negative effect on the development of lungs in young girls, making it harder for them to breathe when they get older.

The Heart and Circulatory System

While the respiratory system brings oxygen into the body, the heart and the blood it pumps carry the oxygen to all the other parts of your body. Once again, cigarette smoking

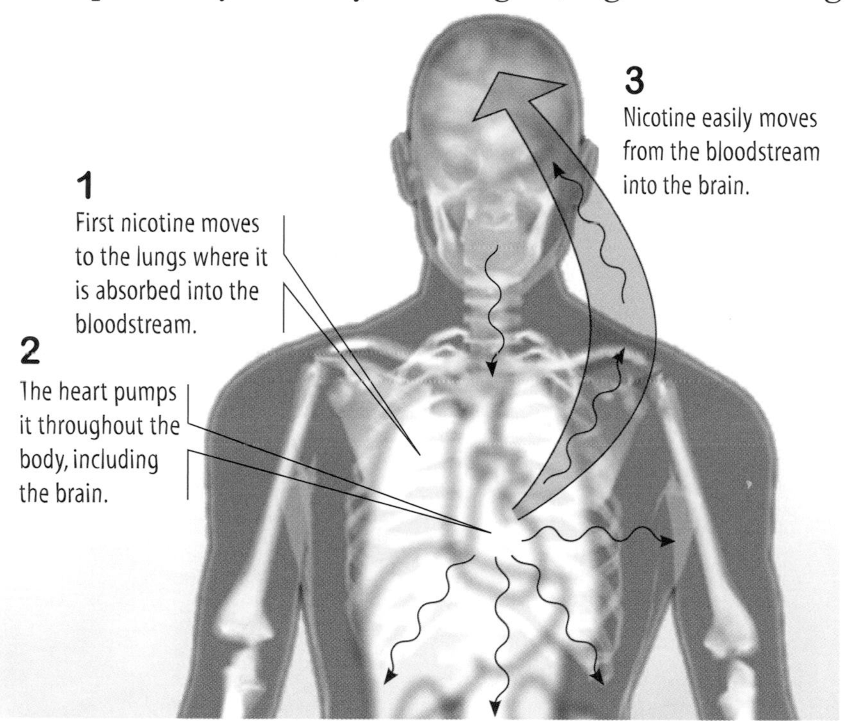

The lungs and heart work together to provide the brain with oxygen, and all those organs are also affected by tobacco smoke.

makes it harder for this circulatory system to do its job properly. Along with the heart, the circulatory system includes the blood vessels—veins, arteries, and capillaries—that carry oxygen and other substances to and from all the body's organs. The heart and lungs are sometimes said to form what is called the **pulmonary** circulation system, while the blood vessels are part of the systemic circulation system.

One of the major health risks from smoking cigarettes is coronary heart disease. Smokers are at least twice as likely than nonsmokers to develop this disease, which is America's number one cause of death. Coronary heart disease can lead to a heart attack, severe chest pain, or erratic heart beats.

Other diseases of the circulatory system linked to cigarettes include:

- Stroke, which is sometimes called a "brain attack"; blood fails to reach certain areas of the brain, which can lead to permanent damage to speech, the ability to think, or move certain parts of the body.
- High blood pressure, which increases the risk of heart attacks.

THE COST OF TOBACCO

Families and governments spend huge amounts of money taking care of the diseases tobacco users develop. Sick smokers or dippers cost businesses, too. Here's a look at some of the figures:

Total medical costs associated with smoking per year:
$96 billion

Amount spent by governments:
almost $68 billion

Amount spent to treat conditions related to secondhand smoke:
almost $5 billion

Government funds given to children who lost at least one parent to smoking:
$2.6 billion

Amount the average business spends on each employee who smokes:
$6,000

Smoking and Pregnancy

Women who smoke and are pregnant must consider how their addiction affects their unborn baby. Studies show that about 15 percent of women smoke while they are pregnant. The children of those women often weigh less than other babies. The more their mothers smoke while pregnant, the less the babies weigh. And the infants of smoking mothers are exposed to nicotine before they're born. When delivered, the infants show signs of being addicted and go through some withdrawal symptoms. The babies of smokers are also at a higher risk of dying while they're still inside their mothers. Once born, they are more likely to experience a condition called sudden infant death syndrome, or SIDS. Children of smoking moms are also more apt to have trouble learning. For a woman who smokes and gets pregnant, her condition signals the perfect time to quit–for her baby's sake, as well as her own.

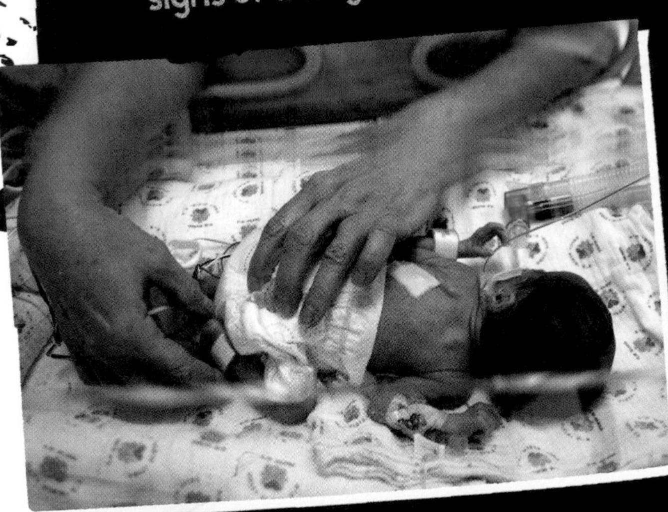

- Blood clots, which can damage organs in the body or lead to heart attacks or strokes.
- Damage to blood vessels in the hands and feet, leading to a condition called peripheral vascular disease. In severe cases, those body parts may need to be removed.

Dangers of Smokeless Tobacco

The list of cancers linked to smoking goes beyond those of the respiratory system to include cancers of the larynx, cervix, stomach, pancreas, and kidney. And smoking is even linked to getting more cavities! But to some young people, the health dangers of tobacco come from smoking it. Using a smokeless type must be safer, right?

Sorry—that idea is a fairy tale. Scientists know that smokeless tobacco presents its own severe health risks. While cigarettes have more carcinogens, smokeless tobacco has at least 28 substances known to cause cancer. The most immediate danger is an increased chance of developing cancer of the mouth. But the risk of developing cancer from chaw or snuff is increased in the esophagus and pancreas too. Smokeless tobacco use has also been linked to heart and gum disease. It also exposes users to more

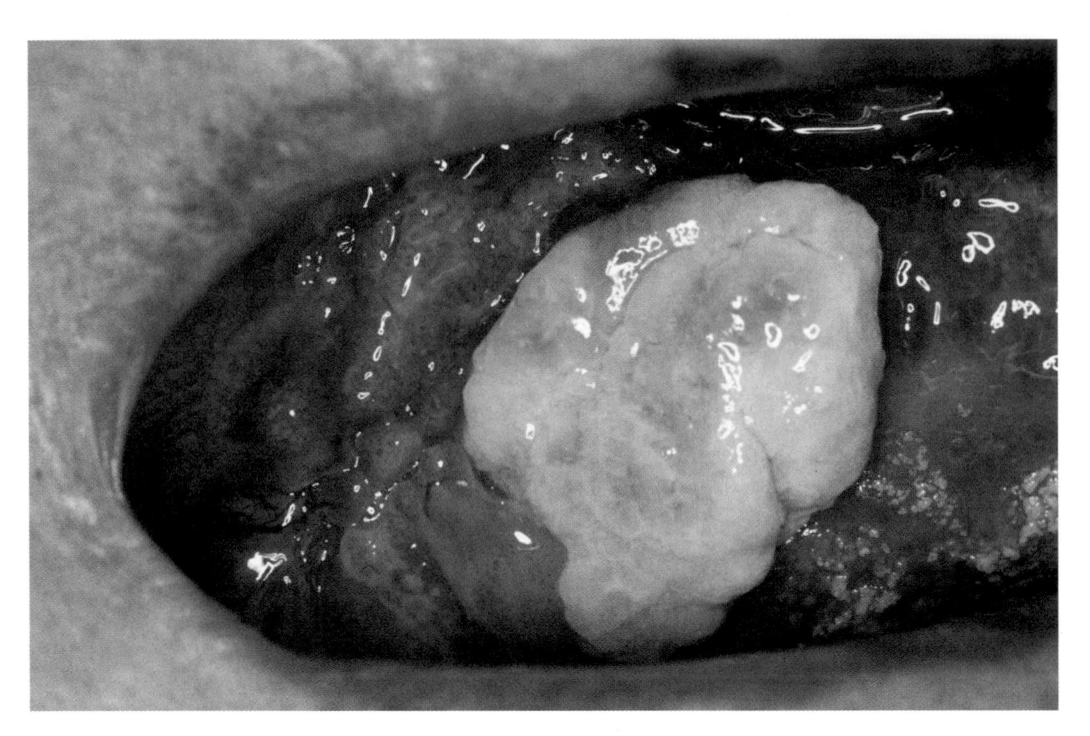

Oral cancer can develop on the lips, tongue, roof of the mouth, gums, and roof of the mouth, as well as inside the cheek.

nicotine, and the nicotine remains in the users' body longer than if they had smoked cigarettes. Then there's the mess—dippers and chewers often have brown stains on their clothes from tobacco juice, and their teeth get brown stains, too. Not a pretty sight for someone hoping to look their best and impress others.

Unfortunately, young people, especially boys, seem to buy into the myth that smokeless tobacco is safer. Government

data from 2011 showed that the number of all smokeless tobacco users was 2.3 percent. But that number was more than double among people between the ages of 18 and 25.

Second- and Thirdhand Dangers

Some smokers say, "It's my body, I can smoke or chew if I want to. I'll take the risk." But with smokers, the reality is their addiction affects others, too. Evidence has grown to show negative effects of secondhand smoke—the tobacco smoke inhaled by nonsmokers who happen to be near smokers. Almost 40,000 deaths each year are linked to people being exposed to secondhand smoke and dying of lung cancer or heart disease. That smoke can also increase the risks of children getting asthma. Even pets are at risk. Dogs and cats that live with smokers are more likely to develop certain cancers and other diseases.

The latest danger associated with cigarette smoking is called thirdhand smoke. You don't need to be a smoker or even around one to face increased health risks. That's because the toxins in the smoke cling to fabrics in clothing, carpeting, and furniture. Over time, the poisons accumulate in those items, and people who come into contact with them are exposed to the poisons. Scientists

Second-hand smoke is also sometimes called passive smoke, and it's particularly harmful to young children because their bodies are still developing.

are just beginning to study the effects of thirdhand smoke, but the dangers seem particularly high for young children.

The smokers themselves are like a walking poison factory, since the smoke gets into their clothes and even their hair. No smoker should think their habit only affects them. Between medical costs and possibly harming others, a smoker is nobody's friend. And the dangers they pose to themselves are even worse.

CHAPTER THREE

In Their Own Words

EVERY DAY, YOU WATCH FAMILY MEMBERS pull out packs of cigarettes and light up, maybe thirty or forty times. You hear them cough and maybe spit up the mucus that fills their lungs. You hear them say, "I'll quit someday," but someday never seems to come.

Or maybe on the ball field, you see a friend put a dip in his mouth during a game. "It's what they do in the big leagues," he tells you. "If players there do it, it must be cool." Meanwhile, as he talks to you, you smell the reek coming from his breath. He doesn't notice—or doesn't care.

It could even be you, thinking about trying tobacco. You read about all the dangers, the addictive quality of nicotine and how easy it is to get hooked, but you don't think it will happen to you. You can smoke that first cigarette, and then some more, and you'll be all right. You're different, somehow—maybe stronger. Or maybe it's just that you're young, you know you have a long time to live. Lung cancer and heart disease and other medical problems connected to tobacco only happen to really old people.

Kids across the country experience these things every day. And for some, seeing how tobacco hurts their friends and families is enough to keep them from ever smoking or dipping. It takes that personal experience to remind us that the 440,000 Americans who die every year because of tobacco is not just a number. It's real people dying—somebody's mother, brother, or friend.

Here are some personal stories from real people. Some are young and some are older but saw the effects of tobacco when they were still kids. All of them realize that tobacco has played a big part in their lives—in a really bad way.

No Will to Quit

Steve M. was really close to his mom, who smoked for many years. When Steve was 17, his mother began on a slow path to death. First she developed a heart virus,

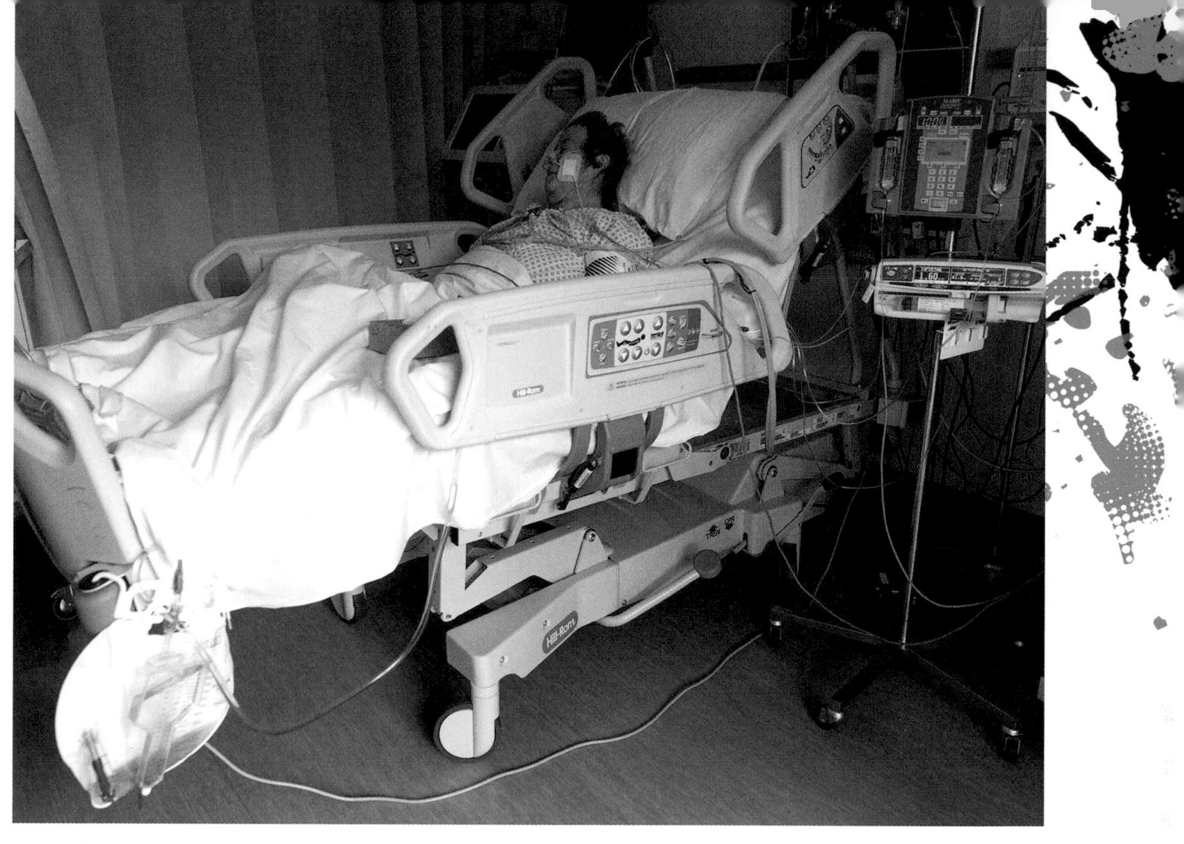

The lifelong effects of smoking cigarettes leaves some people in the intensive care unit of hospitals, suffering from multiple health issues.

which was complicated by the emphysema she developed because of her smoking. That disease makes it harder for oxygen to enter the lungs and for the body to get rid of carbon dioxide. Smoking is the number one cause of emphysema.

As his mother's health grew worse, Steve visited her in the hospital. This is what he remembers from those visits:

> **Her skin** was so gray and leathery. She coughed incessantly and kept saying 'it hurts

so much ... it hurts so much' and then she'd wheel herself and her oxygen tank out to the smoking lounge to light up. It got so bad toward the end that she would crack her ribs from coughing. The **steroids** had so greatly weakened her bones that they were as brittle as twigs. She never tried to quit that I recall. I remember thinking, 'Why doesn't she love me enough to quit?'

Near the end, I winced every time the phone rang. I was in college and waited to get the call. When it finally came I was so relieved. I was heartbroken but relieved. Her suffering was finally over and I no longer had the *not knowing* hanging over me anymore. I found a handwritten note in her things that said: 'Steve ... do not cry so ....' How could I not?

The Trip to the Emergency Room

Lucy G. was also in high school when she saw her mother's smoking habit take its toll. The smoking had already affected Lucy—she was allergic to tobacco smoke, which she didn't learn till years later, and suffered from undiag-

nosed asthma as a kid. She was 16 when she experienced what she calls "one of the most traumatic memories of my life" as she climbed to the top of the stairway in her home. Here's what happened next:

> "[I FOUND] my mom grasping the rail, telling me to get her to the hospital. [I] barely had my license and [was] driving [at] rush hour, her passing out and turning blue in the passenger

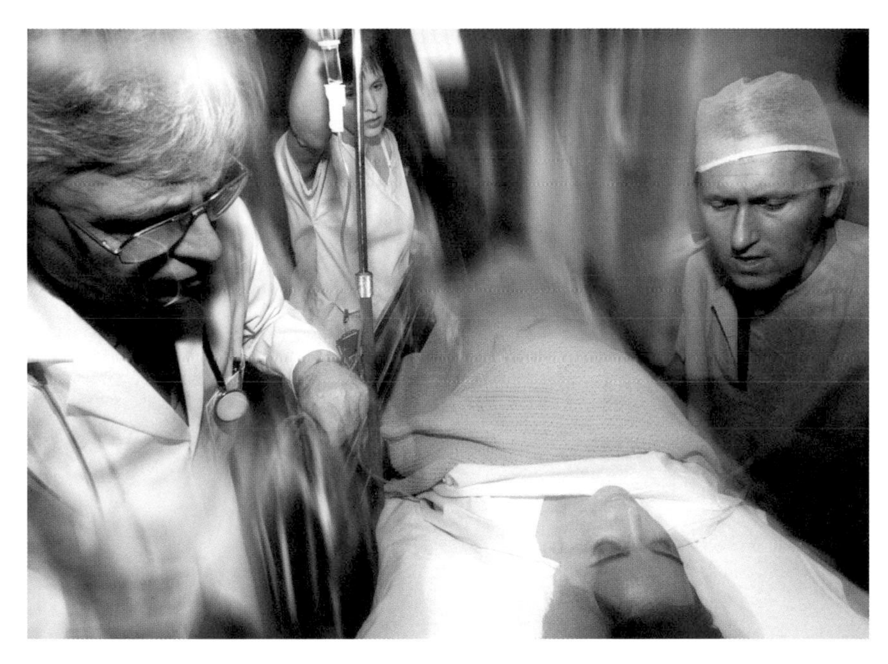

A collapsed lung from smoking or the effects of another undiagnosed tobacco-related disease can mean a trip to the emergency room.

> seat [and can't] give me directions. Got her in the emergency room door and they took her from me and told me to go park the car. Came back in to find them opening up her chest in the hallway, because she had stopped breathing.... Both lungs had collapsed.

Before her mother's health had gotten so bad, Lucy had tried "every way possible to get her to stop smoking ... from breaking all her cigarettes to putting them out as soon as she lit them. Then she almost dies in front of me as a direct result of them ... [I] told my kids ... if I ever caught them with a cigarette, I'd kill them myself. None [of my children] smoke!"

Losing the War

Katie M. grew up in a home where both parents smoked, and many of her friends' parents smoked as well. In the days before tougher antismoking laws, Katie saw her parents light up in restaurants and even on planes. They told Katie that smoking was bad, but they kept right on doing it.

Katie saw the effects firsthand when she was just ten years old. Her father, a former Marine and successful

Children who grow up with parents or other relatives who smoke often try to convince the adult to give up their deadly habit.

businessman, was diagnosed with lung cancer. Within two months, he was dead. She recalls that difficult period in her young life:

> **I WATCHED** him grow weaker and sicker and stroke out from the massive amounts of chemo

he was getting. By Memorial Day weekend of that year, he … was confined to a wheelchair. I never got to say a proper good-bye. He was rushed to the hospital that same weekend for a massive stroke, and he never came home.

It took several years for Katie to really connect her father's death with his cigarette smoking. And once she finally did, she grew mad with her mother.

WHAT BOTHERED me more—and still does—is that my mom continued smoking after his death.… I didn't get how she could continue slowly killing herself and why, as a mother, she would even dream of putting me through the death of another parent.… However, I also have gained a better understanding of what smoking is—a serious addiction.… To this day, my mom continues to suffer from chronic bronchitis and other issues that, though I can't prove it, are likely connected to her smoking. I don't harass her about quitting anymore. I'd

> love her to, but I know she can't and won't. Yet she no longer smokes in front of me and definitely never does in front of my kids.... It is a small victory, but I'd still rather win the war and know my mom's health wasn't in jeopardy. I'd still rather have my dad back.

Feeling the Addiction

Kathy B. was another kid who grew up around smoking parents. She saw her father battle bladder cancer, which may have been linked to his lifelong cigarette habit. Smokers are three times more likely to develop the disease than nonsmokers. Kathy also knew the dangers of tobacco from things she learned in school. But when friends, especially older friends, told her that smoking was cool, Kathy began to smoke, too. She says, "I was still at the age that I thought it was cool simply because I wasn't supposed to do it, and even though I saw how hard it was for my mom to quit I was like, whatever, it won't happen to me.... It took me until the middle of sophomore year to actually get addicted. That was when I remember first actually feeling like I NEEDED to smoke. That's also the last time I can remember going a full day without having at least a little bit of a cigarette.... I haven't even smoked for that long and I can't even count the times I've said 'I'm quitting tomorrow' or 'this is my last cigarette ever.'"

Smokeless Tobacco

As you know, it's not just cigarettes that can kill or cause disease. Smokeless tobacco has also left some kids with incredibly depressing experiences. Take Jason Marsee, who now tells kids, "Imagine your older brother dying in the worst way possible while you watch. That's what happened to me."

Jason's older brother Sean was a star athlete in Ada, Oklahoma, who started using dip and snuff when he was 12. When his mother found out and told him the dangers of smokeless tobacco, Sean argued that his teammates used it, and so did pro athletes, so it must be okay. In reality, Sean would have said anything, since he was already addicted to the nicotine in his snuff. At 18, still a heavy dip user, Sean was diagnosed with mouth, or oral, cancer. Doctors removed half of his tongue. After the surgery, Sean went through **radiation** and **chemotherapy**. One day he asked Jason to go with him for his treatment. Jason recalls, "He asked because he needed me to drive him home. I was fourteen years old,

I didn't have a driver's license, but he would stick his head out the passenger side window and throw up until he passed out." A few weeks later, when the treatments were done, Jason said that Sean was "joking about the fact that they took half his tongue. He's joking about the fact that he won."

But Sean didn't win. The cancer was still in his body and it began to spread. Surgeons removed parts of his neck, chest muscles, and finally his lower jaw. Sean's face was so disfigured at that point, a friend passed out when he came to see him. But all the surgery was too late. Sean died at 19. Even as he went through the painful surgeries, Sean told his mother, "I catch myself thinking, 'I'll just reach over and have a dip.'" Before he died, when he could no longer speak, Sean was asked what he would tell other kids. He wrote on a piece of paper, "Don't do dip." That's the message Jason Marsee still spreads today.

CHAPTER FOUR

Getting Help

SEAN MARSEE CRAVED DIP EVEN AS THE cancer it caused was killing him. Kathy B. still smokes, even knowing her father battled cancer, and knowing the health risks it causes. Meanwhile, each day, thousands of Americans try to quit smoking. The number of people who can do it **cold turkey**, by stopping all at once without any kind of help, is small—between 4 and 7 percent. And most people who quit resume using tobacco and then try to quit again. They may go through this cycle several times before giving up tobacco for good—or remaining hooked for life.

Part of the reason people go back to cigarettes or a chaw is the severe withdrawal symptoms that occur. Without nicotine in their brain, users experience anxiety, trouble sleeping, headaches, and other unpleasant physical conditions. Then there are the mental triggers, the habits or places that smokers associate with smoking—from hanging with friends who smoke to relaxing after a meal. Experiencing the triggers adds to the desire to light up. And with the billions of dollars tobacco companies spend each year advertising their products, users are constantly reminded that cigarettes and smokeless tobacco are out there, waiting to be bought.

But giving up tobacco products has immediate positive results. Smokers can see their blood pressure fall within just 24 hours of quitting. And the longer they go without a cigarette, the better their odds of avoiding heart disease and many cancers. Quitting smoking can add years to a person's life. As the US surgeon general said in a 2010 report, "Quitting gives your body a chance to heal the damage caused by smoking." It also puts money in former smokers' pockets. Regular smokers, who go through a pack a day, spend more than $1,800 every year on their habit. In some states, where cigs are more expensive, it could be twice that! That's a lot of money to spend for a product that only leads to slow death.

Getting Help

For many smokers, kicking their addiction to that powerful drug nicotine requires help. Luckily, for tobacco users of any age, there are plenty of methods for breaking the addiction. Here's a look at some of them.

Nicotine Replacement Therapies (NRT)

You might have seen some former smokers wearing a patch on their arm or frequently chewing gum. Chances are, they're using a nicotine replacement therapy. Nicotine is added to the patch or gum in small doses. With either method, the former smoker gets relief from the withdrawal symptoms of quitting tobacco, while not being exposed to the other harmful chemicals in cigarettes or smokeless tobacco. These NRT products also come as lozenges, an inhaler, and a nasal spray. The goal is to use less and less of the NRT products, until the craving for lighting up or taking a dip is gone. Some of the NRTs require a doctor's prescription, while others can be bought at a drug store. Teens can use NRT products, but the US government

Top: A smoker tries an e-cigarette.

Above: Nicorette is an NRT gum sold openly in stores.

Left: Nicotine patches are often worn on the arm.

Nicotine Anonymous

Years ago, some former alcoholics who finally stopped drinking started the group Alcoholics Anonymous (AA). They wanted to help other heavy drinkers give up the drug. Members used only their first names as they shared their stories of alcohol abuse. AA's goal was to help members stop drinking and then stay sober after. The AA model has been adopted by other drug users seeking to quit, including tobacco users. Nicotine Anonymous (NA) is one example of that. It started in the 1980s and now has meetings in 45 states and more than a dozen foreign countries. Anyone can attend, and there's no cost. Attendees who can afford to give donations do so. As in AA, NA members focus on dealing with their addiction "one day at a time"—the goal is to get through the current day without using tobacco.

suggests that they talk with their doctor or another heath-care provider first. And some studies have shown that using a patch or chewing nicotine is more effective in helping adults quit smoking than in helping teens.

Prescription Drugs

Two drugs originally designed to treat other medical conditions can help tobacco users end their habit: Zyban and Chantix. These drugs are not approved for teens, but for adults they can be effective. Chantix has some of the same effects on the brain as nicotine, so it can ease the symptoms of withdrawal. Zyban simply makes people not want to smoke, though doctors aren't sure how it does this. Both of these drugs can have severe side effects.

Counseling and Treatment Programs

For adults, combining NTR with some sort of smoking **cessation** program leads to more success with quitting. Teens too seem to respond well to some sort of counseling or treatment program. The goals of this kind of treatment include teaching smokers how to avoid their triggers, deal with the stress that comes from trying to quit an addictive drug, and get support from others.

Could a battery-powered cigarette help addicts quit? Some scientists are trying to answer that question.

Can E-Cigs Help You Quit?

Electronic cigarettes, sometimes called e-cigs, have been around for about ten years. They look like cigarettes, but don't contain tobacco-just small amounts of liquid nicotine that are turned into a vapor by an electrical current from a battery. Since there's no tobacco in them, they don't come under laws that regulate cigarette sales. Kids can easily buy them online, and some companies offer the nicotine with flavors that would appeal to kids, like chocolate. Though the idea of any new device that delivers nicotine into the body worries health officials, others say e-cigarettes are safer than regular cigarettes, since they don't contain all the carcinogens found in tobacco. And some people suggest e-cigs could even be another way to help smokers quit. They can slowly reduce the amount of nicotine they inhale, and eventually switch to products that only contain water. Smoking that vapor would satisfy the psychological urge to smoke, once the physical addiction is gone. In 2013, scientists began conducting studies to see if e-cigs were as useful as NRTs in helping people quit. But at the same time, several countries had banned their use. New York State banned them as well.

Counseling for quitting smoking comes in various forms. Some people see a specialist one-on-one, while others go to group sessions at hospitals, schools, or other public settings. People can also get help by phone or through Internet sources. Some of those resources are listed at the end of the book. The U.S. government sponsors the QUIT NOW hotline, which can be reached at 800-784-8669. Callers are directed to their state's tobacco quit line, which offers advice on quitting. If a state doesn't have a quit line, then the caller gets help from the National Cancer Institute. And some of the government programs even have apps that smokers can download to a smartphone or tablet. They help track such things as how long people have gone without smoking and how much money they've saved.

One of the most successful programs for helping teens is called Not on Tobacco (NOT). Several groups, including the American Lung Association, created this program, which is used in many schools and also by community groups. Studies show that about one in six teen smokers who take the NOT classes quit. Others at least reduce their cigarette use. Programs such as NOT show how important it is for kids to get education in small groups to learn about the dangers of smoking and get the support they need to quit.

In some states, kids and teens actively work to keep others from smoking or to quit if they do. Eva M. of New Mexico, says, "Becoming an activist against tobacco inspired me to make the right choices in my life by not using tobacco products myself. I told my mom about the many bad effects tobacco products brings to yourself and others. My mother stopped smoking slowly throughout that year. Now she has little temptation of smoking and is proud of herself for stopping."

Planning to Quit

Once tobacco users decide they really want to quit and learn about the help that's available, there's one more big step to take: choosing a Quit Day. Health experts agree that picking a day, planning for it, and then planning for what could happen afterward are important steps in ending nicotine addiction.

One first step is deciding why quitting is good. If you smoke, you have to believe that you don't want to risk your health, or the health of others with second- and thirdhand smoke. Or maybe you don't want to make others suffer as they watch you die early from a tobacco-related disease. If you dip, you have to want to end the

Saying no if someone offers you a cigarette is the sure way to never get addicted to nicotine.

bad breath and spotted clothes, along with reducing the risk of oral cancer. The truth is, some people don't want to try to quit, because they're so physically or psychologically addicted. But tobacco users who do want to quit realize that they have many good reasons for trying to end their addiction.

The American Cancer Society has some specific suggestions for quitting:

- Pick a Quit Day within the next month. Maybe it's your birthday, or another date that has special meaning for you. Then circle it on the calendar.
- Slowly cut down on the number of cigarettes you smoke each day, unless you decide to go cold turkey.
- Decide on a plan to help you quit by using NRTs, counseling, or both.
- Tell your friends you're quitting and ask for their support. Friends who encourage you to keep smoking are not people you should hang out with. (And if a friend of yours is quitting, you should do what you can to lend your support.)

Every March, kids across the United States and living on military bases around the world take part in Kick Butts Day.

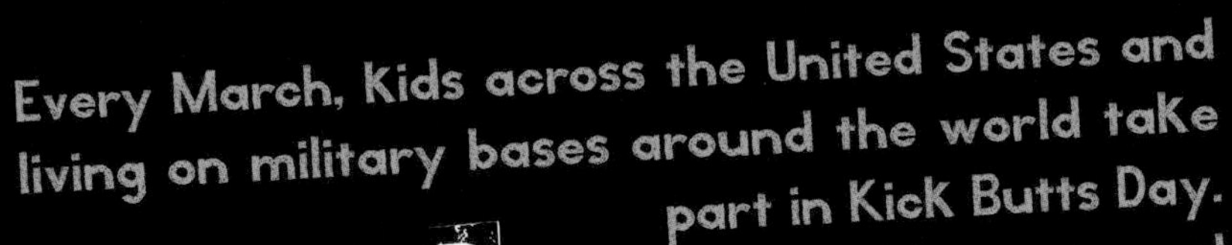

KICK BUTTS DAY

They hold events and activities meant to show the dangers of tobacco use in their communities. The antismoking kids also call for more laws aimed at keeping tobacco out of the hands, mouths, and lungs of American youth. Finally, Kick Butts Day draws attention to the power of the tobacco companies through the money they spend on ads to create the false image that smoking is cool. The kids who take part in Kick Butts Day events want to make it harder for the companies to sell their deadly products to kids.

- Get rid of any cigarettes you might have stashed in hiding places.
- Once your Quit Day comes, try to stay physically active, and avoid the people and situations you connect to smoking. Have healthy snacks around that you can munch on when you get the urge to put something in your mouth. And save the money you used to spend on tobacco to buy yourself a reward.

Knowing the stats on how hard it is to give up tobacco, don't get too down on yourself if you give in and have a smoke or reach for a dip. You just have to pick another Quit Day and put in a little more effort the next time. Giving up tobacco is so important for so many reasons. And of course the best thing is to never begin using it the first place.

Glossary

addictive creating a physical or psychological need to take a drug

additive a chemical or other substance put (or added) into a product, often to change its taste

carcinogens substances that cause cancer

cessation the ending of some act

chaw also chew; smokeless tobacco that comes in long strands or threads and taken in the mouth

chemotherapy chemical treatment used to kill cancer cells

circulatory system parts of the body that transport blood and nutrients

cold turkey stopping the use of an addictive drug all at once

dip moist snuff taken in the mouth

DNA the molecular basis of an individual person's heredity

dopamine a neurotransmitter that controls the brain's response to pleasure

neurotransmitters chemicals that carry signals in the brain

pulmonary relating to the lungs

radiation form of energy that is sometimes used to kill cancer cells

snuff dry tobacco inhaled through the nose

steroids drugs used to reduce the amount of mucous in the lungs, among other conditions

surgeon general a government official who oversees issues relating to public health

tolerance the body's need for more of certain drugs to feel the same effects

withdrawal effects on the body of stopping the use of an addictive drug

Find Out More

Books

Coster, Patience. *Smoking*. Mankato, MN: Arcturus Publishing, 2011.

Marshall Cavendish Reference. *Substance Abuse, Addiction, and Treatment*. New York: Marshall Cavendish, 2012.

Sharp, Katie John. *Teenagers and Tobacco: Nicotine and the Adolescent Brain*. Broomall, PA: Mason Crest, 2009.

Stollers, Veronica, and Elizabeth Keyishian. *Frequently Asked Questions about Smoking*. New York: Rosen Publishing, 2012.

DVDs

Spit This!: The Hazards of Smokeless Tobacco. Human Relations Media, 2010.

This Is Your Brain on Tobacco: A Research Update. Human Relations Media, 2009.

Websites

Smokefree Teen

http://teen.smokefree.gov/default.aspx

This site from the US government offers support for young people looking to quit smoking, as well as examining its health risks.

The Campaign for Tobacco-Free Kids

http://www.tobaccofreekids.org

The website for an organization supporting policies and laws that rcducc thc chanccs of kids and tccns smoking and that encourage current smokers to quit.

Smokeless Tobacco and Cancer

http://www.cancer.gov/cancertopics/factsheet/Tobacco/smokeless

The National Cancer Institute provides this website describing the different forms of smokeless tobacco and the health risks of using them.

Pages in **boldface** are illustrations.

About the Author

MICHAEL BURGAN is the author of more than 250 books for children and young adults, both fiction and nonfiction. He specializes in history but has also written on such subjects as flu vaccines, scientific research, and environmental issues. A graduate of the University of Connecticut with a degree in history, Burgan is also a produced playwright and the editor of *The Biographer's Craft*. He lives in Santa Fe, New Mexico.